Dear

My sweet grandchild, I have so many hopes and dreams for your future. May your life be filled with happiness and adventure. Always remember how much I love you.

Love, tita.

I HOPE YOU ALWAYS FIND SUNSHINE IN YOUR DAY.

MAY YOUR LAUGHTER FILL EVERY ROOM YOU ENTER.

MAY YOUR
HEART BE
AS BIG AS
THE SKY.

I HOPE YOU ALWAYS HAVE A KIND WORD FOR EVERYONE.

MAY YOUR ADVENTURES BE EXCITING AND FUN.

I WISH FOR YOU A LIFE FULL OF HAPPY SURPRISES.

MAY YOUR DREAMS TAKE YOU TO AMAZING PLACES.

I HOPE YOU ALWAYS FEEL SAFE AND LOVED.

MAY YOUR CURIOSITY LEAD YOU TO AMAZING DISCOVERIES.

I WISH YOU A LIFE FILLED WITH PLAYFUL MOMENTS.

MAY YOUR SPIRIT ALWAYS SHINE BRIGHTLY.

I HOPE YOU ALWAYS HAVE SOMEONE TO SHARE YOUR JOY WITH.

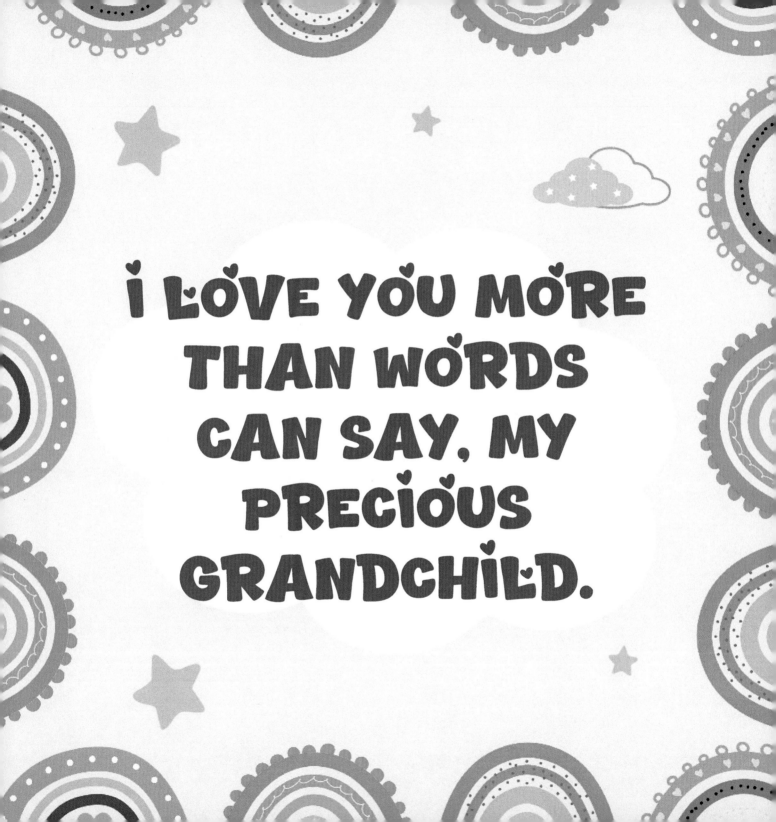

I LOVE YOU MORE THAN WORDS CAN SAY, MY PRECIOUS GRANDCHILD.